DINOSAURS UNLEASHED

2nd Edition

The True Story about Dinosaurs and Humans

Kyle Butt and Eric Lyons
Illustrated by Lewis Lavoie

Dinosaurs Unleashed: The True Story about Dinosaurs and Humans
by Kyle Butt and Eric Lyons

First Edition © 2004
Second Edition © 2008
Apologetics Press, Inc.

ISBN-10: 0-932859-61-5
ISBN-13: 978-0-932859-61-7
Library of Congress: 2003113272

Printed in China

Cover and Artwork by Lewis Lavoie
Layout and Design by
Charles McCown and Rob Baker
Consulting assistance:
Bert Thompson, Ph.D.
Brad Harrub, Ph.D.
Dave Miller, Ph.D.

Apologetics Press, Inc.
230 Landmark Drive
Montgomery, Alabama 36117
U.S.A.

Dedication

To our sons: Andrew Kyle Butt, Elijah Bo Lyons, and Micah Brooks Lyons—who have opened our hearts to the fact that "children are a heritage from the Lord" (Psalm 127:3).

Special thanks to Don Patton and www.Bible.ca for their generous permission to use images from their Web site.

The world of dinosaurs was not a world unknown to man. In the past, he walked with them and ate with them. The first man, Adam, even gave them names (Genesis 2:19-20). Dinosaurs were created by God during the Creation week and for thousands of years they lived upon the Earth as a sign to humans of God's awesome power and creative ability. Unfortunately, evolutionists have tried to convince us that dinosaurs lived millions and millions of years before humans, but that is not true. In this book, we will explore these amazing creatures, and you will discover the true story of how dinosaurs and humans once lived together.

How Fossils are Formed

Once you start reading about dinosaurs, it doesn't take long to discover that most of our information about them comes from fossils. But what are fossils? A fossil is any trace left by something that lived in the past. Animals, plants, and humans have all left many fossils. Some of the most famous fossils are those of the dinosaurs.

How are fossils formed, you might ask? Does every living animal or plant turn into a fossil when it dies? No, every living thing does not become a fossil. In fact, it is very rare for an animal or plant to be fossilized. Let's think about this for a minute. If you see a dead animal on the side of the road, what usually happens to that animal? Does it turn into a fossil? No, it doesn't. Most of the time, scavengers such as buzzards or opossums carry it off. Also, bugs, worms, bacteria, and enzymes cause the animal to rot and decay so that, eventually, no trace of it remains.

However, that is not always the case. In some instances, an animal or a plant gets buried very quickly. No scavengers can find it, and oxygen, which is a major cause of decay, cannot get to it. Even in this protected environment, much of the soft tissue (such as fur and skin) decays. But the harder structures (like bones and teeth) last longer. Water that contains minerals, such as silica, seeps through the bones and teeth. The animal's

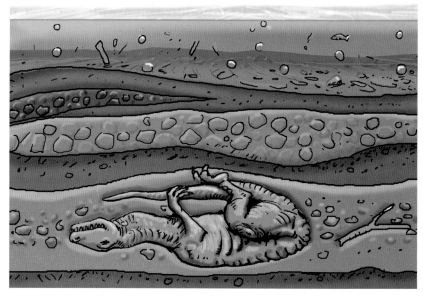

bones begin to decay, but the minerals in the water start to fill in the decaying areas. Eventually, minerals replace the entire bone or tooth. When the fossil is discovered years later, the original bones have turned into mineralized rock. This is one of the ways fossils are formed.

In some cases, the animal is buried and decays entirely, but when it does, it leaves a hollow mold that preserves the shape and size of its bones. Another type of fossilization occurs when insects like mosquitoes or flies get trapped in tree sap called amber.

Some people think that this process of fossilization must take thousands or even millions of years, but that is not the case. In fact, a miner's hat has been found that had been totally fossilized (turned into rocky mineral). Also, a western boot was found that had a bone inside it that had fossilized. The boot, however, had not fossilized, which shows that some materials, such as bone, fossilize better than other materials, like leather or animal skin.

Courtesy of www.Bible.ca

When we find fossils of dinosaurs, we often find them in huge piles all jumbled together. These large piles of dinosaurs must have been buried very quickly. What do you think could have buried many huge dinosaurs at the same time all around the world? One good answer would be the Flood of Noah. If local floods today can cause whole roads and houses to be buried, just imagine what a worldwide flood could do! When we look at the "record of the rocks," we find that fossils do not take millions of years to form, and that the Flood of Noah's day could easily have created many of the fossils we see today.

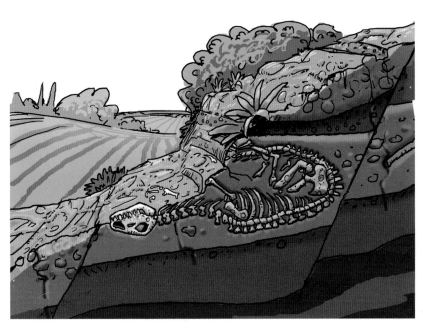

Buried Treasure

Most of the time, we think about buried treasure such as gold or silver that is buried in a wooden chest. But there are other treasures buried in the ground. Fossils are buried treasures that can be worth millions of dollars and can change the way we think about the past. Wouldn't it be exciting to walk through your backyard and spot something sticking up from the ground that looked like a dinosaur fossil? What would you do? How would you dig it up? Would the fossil break as you tried to get it out of the ground? Would you send it to a museum, or get to keep it at your house?

Once a fossil is discovered, there are many things that must be done in order to make sure that it is dug up properly. In fact, scientists known as paleontologists are trained to know exactly how to remove fossils from the ground. Paleontology is the study of ancient life (*paleo* comes from the Greek word meaning "ancient" or "old," and *ology* means "the study of").

Paleontologists take their job very seriously—and they work very slowly and carefully. When fossils are found, the location is marked on a map. Then, the scientists begin to take pictures of the entire area. Sometimes, huge bulldozers are used to remove large mounds of dirt. Other times, the fossils are embedded in rock layers. Paleontologists use picks, hammers, and chisels to chip away at the rock around the fossils, being very careful to protect the actual fossil. Digging up fossils can take many years. In some cases, the fossils are covered with a type of glue to keep them from falling apart. If the fossils are very large, the researchers often put plaster casts around them in order to protect them when they are moved. Then, large cranes can be used to lift them out of the dig site.

As each fossil is being removed, scientists make careful notes and photographs that show which bones are connected. These photographs and notes are crucial to the outcome of the find. Many times, the bones will be shipped to a busy museum where they may not be put together for several years. If the notes and photographs were not done right, then the fossils would be almost impossible to assemble.

Often, more than one museum would like to display the fossil find. In that case, artificial molds of the bones can be made of plaster. Most of the dinosaur skeletons we see in museums today are made from

a dog. From studying dinosaur fossils, we learn where they lived, how big they were, and countless other exciting things.

However, since we find only fossils and a few remains of the dinosaurs, there are many things we cannot know. Much of the information we have about dinosaurs has come from looking at their bones, and trying to decide how dinosaurs would have moved, hunted, eaten, and lived. In the years to come, scientists will probably find more dinosaur fossils, and learn that some of their ideas about dinosaurs were exactly right—while other ideas were wrong. But one thing that will not change is the fact that God created these creatures alongside humans only a few thousand years ago. Let's explore the evidence.

plaster molds and are not the actual fossils. The next time you walk through a museum, remember all the steps that were taken to get those fossils there. And, if you happen to find some important fossils one day, take special care of them. Who knows? They might get to go in a museum someday.

Fossils are exciting because they tell us about creatures that lived in the past. Dinosaurs are one group of these fascinating creatures. Dinosaurs capture the attention of kids and adults. Scientists learn interesting facts about these animals by studying their fossils. Some dinosaurs ate meat, while others ate vegetation. Some dinosaurs were ten times as big as an elephant, and others were about the size of

Dinosaur Hunters

Othniel Marsh

Although many of the original scientific finds of dinosaur bones were in England, the first great hunt for dinosaurs started in the United States. In the 1860s, Othniel Marsh and Edward Cope started a friendly "contest" to see who could find the most dinosaur fossils. Both men were very wealthy, and they had the time and money to spend on such a project. But their friendly game soon turned into a bitter rivalry. By the 1870s, both men were racing to beat the other one to dinosaur fossils in the western part of the United States. It was said that the race became so fierce that bones were stolen and fossils were destroyed so that the opposing side would not find them. This bitter rivalry did not end until 1897, when Edward Cope died.

After all the smoke had cleared and the feud had ended, several new species of dinosaurs had been discovered. Dinosaurs such as the *Stegosaurus*, *Allosaurus*, and *Triceratops* were just a few of the more famous finds by the two great dinosaur hunters. Their bitter fight brought dinosaurs to the attention of the United States and the rest of the world. It cost Marsh and Cope hundreds of thousands of dollars and countless hours, but their feud helped make dinosaurs famous.

Edward Cope

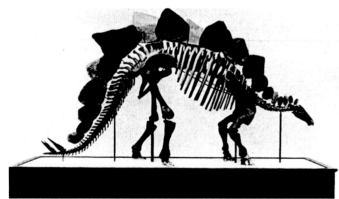

Stegosaurus

Triceratops

6

MEGALOSAURUS

Some dinosaurs are well known for their huge size or massive teeth. Others become famous because their fossils were found in a certain spot, or because their fossils are very well preserved. So why is *Megalosaurus* famous? *Megalosaurus* was the first dinosaur in modern times to be scientifically named. In 1676-1677, a man named Robert Plot found a fossil of a *Megalosaurus* thighbone. However, Mr. Plot thought that the bone came from a giant human being. Then, in the early 1800s, William Buckland found several fossils near Oxford, England. Those fossils included a lower jaw, some teeth, part of the hipbone, and parts of a backbone. After studying the fossils for several years, Buckland wrote a paper about them in 1824, and he named the animal *Megalosaurus*, meaning "great lizard." He was the first man to scientifically name a specific dinosaur. Because of this achievement, today the dinosaur's full name is *Megalosaurus bucklandii,* in honor of William Buckland.

Megalosaurus was a carnivore (meat eater) that could grow to be about 30 feet long and 10 feet high (about as tall as a basketball goal). It probably weighed about 1 ton (2,000 pounds). It had two short arms with three sharp claws on each hand. *Megalosaurus'* powerful jaws and sharp teeth would have helped it survive. With long legs and three-clawed feet, this creature was most likely a good hunter. Fossilized bones and footprints have been found in Europe, South America, Africa, and Asia.

The top picture shows what scientists thought Megalosaurus *looked like when its bones were first discovered. The parts in red show all the bones they had to work with. The bottom picture shows a modern version of* Megalosaurus. *See how much ideas have changed!*

IGUANODON

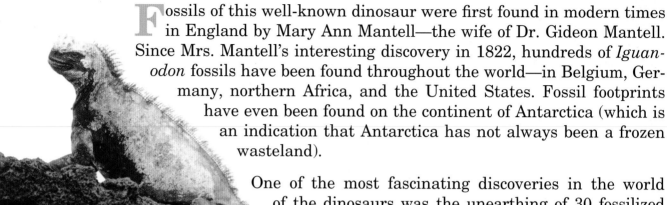

ossils of this well-known dinosaur were first found in modern times in England by Mary Ann Mantell—the wife of Dr. Gideon Mantell. Since Mrs. Mantell's interesting discovery in 1822, hundreds of *Iguanodon* fossils have been found throughout the world—in Belgium, Germany, northern Africa, and the United States. Fossil footprints have even been found on the continent of Antarctica (which is an indication that Antarctica has not always been a frozen wasteland).

Iguanas like this one are many times smaller than the dinosaur known as Iguanodon.

One of the most fascinating discoveries in the world of the dinosaurs was the unearthing of 30 fossilized *Iguanodon* skeletons in a Belgian coal mine in 1878. Because so many *Iguanodons* were found in one place, scientists believe that these dinosaurs lived mainly in herds. Many theories have arisen as to why this massive dinosaur graveyard exists alongside (and underneath) tons of fossilized plants that turned into coal. Though we may never know for sure, it is quite possible that the worldwide Flood of Noah's day was the cause of this graveyard, as well as other dinosaur graveyards around the world.

Iguanodon (meaning "iguana tooth") was given its name because its teeth were like those of an iguana, but much larger. This creature grew to be about 30 feet long and weighed an estimated 4½ tons. It had a strong, rigid tail and cone-like spiked thumbs. It also had a turtle-like, toothless beak at the front of its mouth that was very helpful in picking vegetation. Once the vegetation was in its mouth, *Iguanodon* would then proceed to grind the leaves with numerous ridged teeth that lined the sides of the jaws. Research has shown that this dinosaur probably was capable of walking on either two or four legs.

The Iguanodon's thumb spike was first thought to have been a horn on the creature's nose. This picture shows the actual size of the spike.

8

T. rex is also losing its status as the largest meat eater. Today, fossils of at least two other meat-eating dinosaurs have been found that are larger than *Tyrannosaurus rex*. In 1995, scientists found fossils of a *Giganotosaurus* (meaning giant southern lizard) in the country of Argentina. *Giganotosaurus* was a monster of a meat eater that is estimated to have outweighed *T. rex* by almost 5,000 pounds. Also, in the Sahara Desert, a huge *Carcharodontosaurus* (shark-toothed reptile) was found with a skull about 5 feet 4 inches long. This meat-eating machine measured about 45 feet from end to end. Another carnivore rivaling *T. rex* is the *Spinosaurus*. *Spinosaurus* was probably longer than *T. rex*, with a huge sail on its back, making it look even larger. However, it was lighter than *T. rex*, and had a thinner mouth and head.

With all the fossil hunters working today, there is no telling what new creature might turn up next. But *T. rex* will always hold a special place in the hearts of dinosaur lovers all over the world as the first terrifying "king tyrant lizard."

Actual size of a T. rex *claw from one of its feet.*

GIGANOTOSAURUS

Bigger than *T. rex* or *Spinosaurus*, *Giganotosaurus* reigns, for the present, as possibly the largest meat eater ever to walk the planet. The name *Giganotosaurus* means "giant southern lizard," and giant it was. Its skull alone was almost six feet long, with a massive mouth filled with razor-sharp teeth the size of steak knives. *Giganotosaurus* was about 3 feet longer and 2,000 pounds heavier than "Sue," the largest *T. rex* skeleton ever found. At 46-48 feet long, weighing an estimated 8 tons, and standing anywhere from 12-17 feet tall at the hips, this carnosaur (meat-eating dinosaur) was the biggest, but maybe not the "baddest." Even though it was larger than *T. rex*, it looks like *Giganotosaurus* had a smaller brain (about the size of a banana). In addition, its teeth were narrower than the tyrant lizard's, and

it probably did not have jaw muscles as powerful as *T. rex*. However, its heavy frame and skull do look very much like those of *T. rex*, yet its arms had three-fingered "hands," unlike *T. rex*'s two-fingered "hands." Let's just say if these two animals ever got in a fight, no one knows who would win, but it would be best not to be anywhere close to the action. *Giganotosaurus* walked on its two powerful hind legs in a manner very similar to the other large meat eaters. In the early 1990s, a man named Ruben D. Carolini found the bones of *Giganotosaurus* in Argentina. In honor of his discovery, the huge dinosaur has been named *Giganotosaurus carolini*. The way things are going for fossils hunters these days, *Giganotosaurus* may not stay at the top of the dinosaur "hall of fame" for very long.

13

SPINOSAURUS

Rivaling *T. rex* as one of the largest meat eaters ever to roam the Earth, *Spinosaurus* has grabbed the attention of dinosaur lovers around the globe. A few years ago, *Spinosaurus* gained international fame when it battled *T. rex* in the hit movie, *Jurassic Park III*. At 48-50 feet long and weighing an estimated 4-6 tons, this huge carnosaur would have been a sight to behold. The long spines (called neural spines) protruding from its back were its most distinguishing feature. These spines could reach a height of about six feet. Many people believe that a huge skin "sail" was attached to the spines. This sail might have been used to regulate temperature, attract mates, or scare off other dinosaurs. *Spinosaurus* (meaning "spine lizard" or "thorn lizard") gets its name from these neural spines. It probably walked on its two powerful hind legs. It also had two arms that were longer than those of *T. rex*. Because of the length of its arms, some people think *Spinosaurus* might have walked on all four legs some of the time. Its skull looked like that of a crocodile (only much bigger), and it had many long, sharp, straight teeth. *Spinosaurus* could reach an estimated height of 18½ feet tall (if you include the spines). Unfortunately, not much is known about this creature because very few fossils of it have been uncovered. A bombing that occurred during World War II destroyed the best fossils ever found, which were discovered in Egypt and Morocco.

ALLOSAURUS

People have described this extinct creature as "big, bad, and a little different." The name *Allosaurus* comes from two Greek words that mean "different lizard." Although *Allosaurus* looked like other carnosaurs (meat-eating dinosaurs like *T. rex* and *Giganotosaurus*), its unusual backbones (being lighter than those of other dinosaurs) were what gave this creature its name.

With a head about three feet long and a mouth packing nearly 70 sharp teeth that were 2-4 inches in length, this carnosaur was surely one of the most feared animals on Earth. He could reach lengths of 40 feet and heights of 16 feet, while weighing up to 4½ tons. Although his arms were very short (compared to the rest of his body), on the end of each finger was a sharp claw that grew up to 6 inches long. Evidence that this fierce creature occasionally fought large plant eaters comes from *Apatosaurus* backbones that have been found with *Allosaurus* teeth marks on them. It is pretty unlikely that these markings are the result of *Allosaurus* and *Apatosaurus* playing a friendly game of tag.

In the great dinosaur graveyards near the Colorado/Utah border, about 5,000 *Allosaurus* bones from nearly 55 individual *Allosaurs* have been found buried together.

Scientists are uncertain what caused this large-scale destruction, but the best explanation for this dinosaur graveyard (as well as many of the dinosaur graveyards throughout the world) is that they are the result of the global Flood of Noah's day.

Apatosaurs

Seismosaurus

COMPSOGNATHUS

Even though many of the extinct reptiles were monstrous creatures, *Compsognathus* was only about the size of a large rooster. This little guy weighed just six pounds and grew to be only 3 feet long from head to tail.

His name means "pretty jaw." The small jaw was filled with many small, sharp teeth that probably were used to eat small animals like lizards or rodents. [Rodents would have been around at that time, because dinosaurs like *Compsognathus* were made on day six of Creation—the same day as rodents.] Only two fossilized skeletons of *Compsognathus* have ever been found. In one case, the skeleton of a small lizard was found inside the fossilized stomach region of one of these creatures. This dinosaur's ability to catch little lizards probably indicates that he could move around very swiftly on his skinny legs and three-toed feet.

Deinonychus

Although *Deinonychus* stood just a little taller than the average human, he was one dinosaur you would not want to upset. He had large eyes, two slender, strong legs, a rigid tail, and powerful jaws filled with sharp, serrated teeth. Scientists have been most impressed with the intimidating claws of *Deinonychus*.

After taking a close look at this extinct reptile, it does not take long to understand why he was given a name meaning "terrible claw." He had three fingers on each hand and four toes on each foot—all with sharp claws. One toe was short (scientists believe it probably never even touched the ground), while two toes were used for walking and running. It was the other toe on each foot of *Deinonychus*, however, that makes this dinosaur stand out above the others. One toe on each foot was equipped with the "terrible claw"— a powerful, five-inch long, sickle-like claw that was most likely used to tear into or hold onto food. Fossilized bones of *Deinonychus* have been found in Montana, Wyoming, and Utah.

24

This "terrible claw" is shown at actual size.

TROODON

Due to its large brain, many people think that *Troodon* might have been the smartest dinosaur ever to roam the Earth. This small predator could grow to be about 6 feet long and was about 3 feet high at the hips. It weighed about 130 pounds, about the size of an adult human female. *Troodon*'s name means "wounding tooth." This name comes from its large, serrated teeth that probably were used to eat small lizards, rodents, or other animals. Another weapon in *Troodon*'s arsenal was a sharp, sickle-like claw on the second toe of each foot. This claw may have been used to wound and kill large prey, and it could have been used for defense or in battles over mating rights.

With hollow bones and long legs, *Troodon* most likely would have been very quick on its feet. Its long, slender neck and big eyes would have helped it spot prey easily. In fact, its eyes were so big that some have suggested that *Troodon* may have been nocturnal (hunting at night) because of its terrific eyesight. This agile predator, with a mouth full of serrated teeth, claws that could grip, and a sickle-like claw, would have been a terror to smaller creatures of its time.

Velociraptor

After examining the fossils of *Velociraptor* (which have been found in the countries of Mongolia, Russia, and China), you will likely notice how much this extinct creature resembles the North American dinosaur named *Deinonychus*. Both dinosaurs had sharp teeth, muscular legs, a stiff tail, and fierce claws. *Velociraptor*, however, was smaller than *Deinonychus*. It had a long snout that was low, flat, and narrow, which was very different from that of other dinosaurs, and its fierce claw was not quite as large as that of *Deinonychus*.

Although the producers of the movie *Jurassic Park* portrayed *Velociraptor* as being a fairly large dinosaur, scientists who have studied the fossilized remains of *Velociraptor* believe that he was no larger than a Great Dane dog—about 400% smaller than the size it was portrayed in *Jurassic Park*. It is believed that he was a quick and agile predator. In 1971, a *Velociraptor* was found fossilized alongside a *Protoceratops*. Apparently, the two dinosaurs died while in a vicious fight. The *Velociraptor* was found with one of his claws gripping the crown of the *Protoceratops*.

26

Oviraptor

Weighing in at only 80 pounds and reaching only 3 or 4 feet tall, the *Oviraptor* was about the height and weight of an average German Shepherd dog. However, at 6-8 feet long, it would have been about 3 feet longer. The name *Oviraptor* means "egg thief." This little reptile was first found in 1924 very near a nest of eggs. Scientists then thought that the eggs belonged to a *Protoceratops*, and that the *Oviraptor* was stealing the eggs. The crushed skull of the fossilized "egg thief" was thought to have been an injury it received while trying to steal the eggs.

However, scientists are learning that their "egg thief" might not be such a thief after all. In southern Mongolia, an *Oviraptor* fossil was found near a nest of eggs. But this time, scientists found embryos (baby dinosaurs) in the eggs that were *Oviraptor* babies. As it turns out, the *Oviraptor* probably was not stealing eggs at all. Instead, it was probably protecting its own eggs. Isn't it funny how often our first thoughts about things (especially dinosaurs) turn out to be wrong when more evidence appears?

Oviraptor had long legs and was lightweight. It walked on two legs and had two arms with long, slender "hands." Each "hand" had three claws about 3 inches long. Some people think that it could have run as fast as an ostrich—about 40 miles per hour. The *Oviraptor* had a short beak with no teeth, a crest on top of its snout, and very large eyes for its size. We do not know exactly what this dinosaur ate. It might have been an omnivore–an animal that could eat both plants and smaller animals.

PACHYCEPHALOSAURUS

If you can imagine a reptile that was about 17 feet long, 10 feet high, and had what looked like a huge bowling ball on top of its head, then you can imagine a *Pachycephalosaurus*. Its name means "thick-headed lizard" and comes from the huge, bony dome on top of the dinosaur's head. *Pachycephalosaurus* walked on two powerful hind legs. It had short forearms with five-clawed fingers. It was probably a herbivore, eating softer plants, seeds, and fruit with its small, sharp teeth. *Pachy's* huge skull could grow to be ten inches thick, but it housed a very small brain. Short, bony spikes stuck out of the back of this dome, and bony "bumps" grew around the sides of the skull.

For a long time, many people thought that these creatures might have butted heads like bighorn sheep do. However, there might be some problems with this idea. First, although the bone on top of its head was thick, it was porous (filled with holes) and more fragile than at first thought. It might not have been strong enough to handle that much force. Second, if a pair of these dinosaurs was to head-butt, the dome-shaped skull probably would have caused them to glance off one another and be terribly injured by the spikes in the back of the skull. Actually, we do not know what the thick skull of this creature was used to do. Maybe it was used to charge the rib cages of dinosaurs like *T. rex*. and *Spinosaurus*.

Skeletons of *Pachycephalosaurus* are very rare. As you can imagine, most of the time only the skull is found. Some people think fossils might be rare because this dinosaur lived in mountainous regions where it would be difficult to fossilize things. For whatever reason, we know very little about this amazing animal. Maybe in the years to come, we will find more clues to help us understand this dinosaur.

PARASAUROLOPHUS

It would be hard to miss this large dinosaur with a five-foot crest on its head. Although *Parasaurolophus* may not have been one of the most common dinosaurs, it certainly was one of the most unique. This dinosaur could grow to be 33 feet long, 16 feet high, and weigh almost 2 tons. It was in the group of dinosaurs called the hadrosaurs (which means "bulky lizards"). Hadrosaurs are often known as the "duck-billed" dinosaurs because they had a bill like a duck. Behind this bill were hundreds of small teeth used to grind up plants. Many of the fossils of hadrosaurs show that some of them had webbed hands and were probably good swimmers. Also, some of the hadrosaurs, like *Parasaurolophus*, had bony crests on their heads. What did *Parasaurolophus* do with this crest, which was as tall as an average fourth-grade child? Scientists don't know for sure. Inside the crest were hollow tubes attached to the nostrils and mouth. It is possible that the creature might have used the crest as a type of horn, producing sounds to attract mates or to scare off predators. Some scientists made replicas of the crest and recorded sounds they think that it might have made. The creature also may have used the bony crest to spit out some type of gas or other harmful substance to protect itself, especially since its fossils indicate that it had very few other defenses. Furthermore, the crest might have helped the animal to smell things from far away. Whatever the crest did, it was probably very important to this dinosaur. It might have been able to see well and run, but it also may have made a good meal for *T. rex* or *Giganotosaurus*.

LAMBEOSAURUS

Lambeosaurus was one of the biggest duck-billed dinosaurs. It could grow to be about 45 feet long and 20 feet high, and it weighed 5-6 tons. Like the other hadrosaurs, it had a toothless bill, with many small cheek teeth behind its bill that were used to grind the plants it ate. The name *Lambeosaurus* means "Lambe's lizard." It was given this name because the Canadian fossil hunter, Lawrence Lambe, discovered this creature. *Lambeosaurus* is best known for the large crest on its skull. This crest was shaped somewhat like a hatchet, and was hollow. The nasal passages of *Lambeosaurus* ran through the crest, much like those of the *Parasaurolophus*. No one knows the exact purpose of the crest. It might have been used to enhance the creature's sense of smell, to allow the dinosaur to make amplified noises, or to act as a "breathing chamber" when the animal swam under water.

Edmontosaurus

As a "duck-billed" dinosaur, *Edmontosaurus* probably traveled in herds (we think this because large numbers of fossils have been found jumbled together). It was a herbivore that ate things like pine needles, leaves, and other plants. Conifer needles have been found in the stomach of a fossilized *Edmontosaurus*. Its name means "Edmonton lizard." It was given this name because it was found in the Edmonton rock formation in Alberta, Canada.

Edmontosaurus ranked as one of the biggest duck-billed dinosaurs, since it could grow to a length of about 43 feet, a height of 20 feet, and a weight of about 4 tons (8,000 pounds). With two large back legs and two smaller front legs, this dinosaur could probably walk on all four legs or balance on its two back legs. This creature had a large head (about the size of a horse's head) and a toothless bill that was used to snip leaves and twigs. Behind this bill, inside its cheeks, were 45-60 rows of jaw teeth. Each row could have over ten teeth in it, giving the *Edmontosaurus* cheeks that could contain 500-1,000 teeth. (Wouldn't you hate to get your hand caught in there?)

With very few defenses, this plant eater probably provided many good meals for dinosaurs like *T. rex*. In fact, remains of *Edmontosaurus* bones have been found in the droppings of *T. rex*. Another fossil of *Edmontosaurus* has a "bite" out of its spine that looks like it could have come from a *T. rex*. Large numbers of *Edmontosaurus* fossils have been found in Alberta, Canada. Also, two mummified *Edmontosaurus* fossils found in Wyoming show that the animal had leathery skin.

Corythosaurus

This duck-billed dinosaur's name means "helmet lizard." It was given this name because it had a bony crest on the top of its head that looked like a narrow helmet. (See picture on the left.) This creature ate an abundance of plants, which helped it grow to be about 30 feet tall and weigh about 10,000 pounds.

TRICERATOPS

The head of this creature was one of the largest that any land animal ever possessed, with a skull that could reach a length of ten feet. The *Triceratops* (meaning "three-horned face") ranks among the most familiar dinosaurs of all time. As a herbivore (plant eater), it had a parrot-like beak that could chop down small trees. It also had grinding teeth in the back of its jaw to grind the tough stalks. On the top of its beak was a small horn, and just behind that were two large horns that could reach 3 feet in length. These horns probably had all sorts of uses. They could have been used to pull down trees and branches for the dinosaur to eat. The menacing horns would also serve as good defensive weapons against predators such as the *Spinosaurus*. Just behind the horns was a bony "frill" that could grow to be about 7 feet wide. *Triceratops* might have used its horns and frill to fight for mates, much like deer and other animals do today.

From what we can estimate, this creature, which was the size of a dump truck, would have weighed about 14,000 pounds (7 tons), reached heights of 9½ feet tall, and grown to be 26-30 feet long. It walked on four legs, had a fairly large brain, and a short, pointy tail. *Triceratops* is the heaviest, most well-known member of the family of ceratopsian dinosaurs (meaning "horned faces"). Fossil beds have been found where several cera-topsian bodies were jumbled together in one place, suggesting that they, too, traveled in herds. In 1887, Othniel Marsh found the first *Triceratops* horn, but he thought it was the horn of a buffalo. In 1888, he found a complete skull, and the next year he named the creature *Triceratops*. Most *Triceratops* fossils have been found in Canada and the United States.

STYRACOSAURUS

Some dinosaurs are not as popular as *T. rex* or *Triceratops*, but they are just as interesting. *Styracosaurus* (meaning "spiked lizard") is one of those dinosaurs that receives little attention, but its spiked frill is quite an eye catcher. This beast grew to be 18 feet long and 6 feet high, weighing about 3 tons. Its neck frill was covered with long spikes. A 2½-foot-long horn was attached to its snout, and it had two small horns above its eyes. As with the other ceratopsians, the horns were probably used as an effective defense against predators, or as weapons to fight for a mate. It was a stocky plant eater that walked on four legs. It also probably roamed in herds. One group of fossils found in Alberta, Canada provided bones from about 100 individuals and at least one complete skeleton.

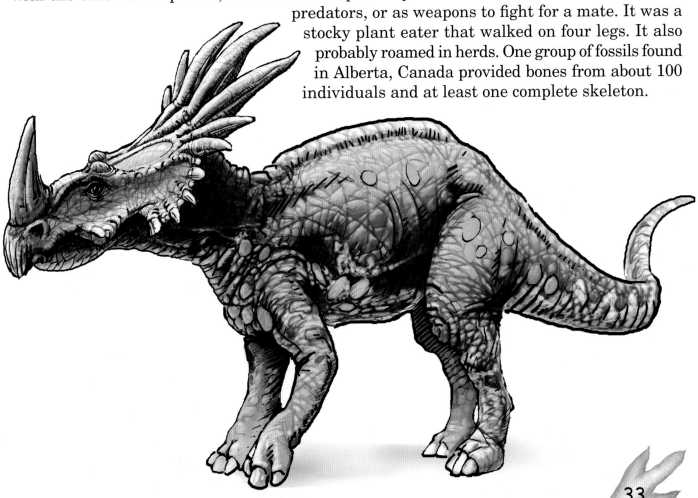

STEGOSAURUS

Looking like a heavily armored tank with spikes on its tail and large plates along its spine, the *Stegosaurus* is one of the most famous dinosaurs of all time. The name *Stegosaurus* (meaning "covered lizard" or "roof lizard") comes from the plates that stick out from its neck, back, and tail. Until 1992, scientists did not know how these plates were arranged, but in that year a discovery showed that they stuck up. The ones directly in the middle of the back were probably the tallest. They could reach heights of 2½ feet.

No one knows exactly what *Stegosaurus* used its plates to do. The bones of the plates had lots of holes in them for blood vessels. This would have made them somewhat fragile. Because of this, scientists think that the plates might have been used to regulate the body temperature of the dinosaur. Also, blood might have been pumped into the plates, causing them to change colors in order to scare off predators or attract mates. Maybe in the future we will find fossil evidence that can tell us more about these plates.

Even if the plates weren't used for protection, that did not make *Stegosaurus* an easy target for meat eaters. At the end of *Stegosaurus'* tail were up to eight large spikes that could grow to be 3 feet long. These spikes would have made any carnivore think twice before moving in for a Stegoburger. As a further defense, *Stegosaurus* had bones under its neck that acted like armor for its throat.

Stegosaurus was a herbivore with a long, narrow head and a toothless beak. Behind the beak, it had several small teeth. Its two front legs were short and had five toes. Its back legs were straighter and much longer, with only three toes. Because of its long back legs, some people think that this dinosaur might have been able to rear up on its back legs and tail in order to eat higher vegetation from tall bushes and trees. *Stegosaurus* could grow to be about 26-30 feet long (almost as long as a school bus) and weigh approximately 6,800 pounds. Although it was quite large, it had a brain only about the size of a golf ball, so it probably was not the most intelligent animal in the woods. Fossils of *Stegosaurus* have been found in the United States, China, India, and many other places.

ANKYLOSAURUS

Unlike many dinosaurs its size, it seems that *Ankylosaurus* had few reasons to be concerned about carnivorous (meat-eating) dinosaurs. He grew to be about 30 feet long, 5 feet wide, 4 feet tall at the hips, and weighed as much as a full-grown hippopotamus (4 tons). It was not *Ankylosaurus'* size, however, that kept him from being a regular afternoon snack for the much larger carnivores like *Giganotosaurus* or *Allosaurus*.

Meaning "fused lizard" [because the armor plates on its back were "fused" (or connected) together], *Ankylosaurus* could protect itself simply by crouching close to the ground. In this way, it would be almost completely protected by its armored back, which was covered with several horn-like spikes. Even though *Ankylosaurus'* underside was not "armored" like its topside, it had little reason to be concerned. Attackers would find it very difficult to turn this creature over for two reasons: (1) the spikes that extended along its back would have discouraged attempts to roll it over; and (2) its heavy body was so near to the ground. (Thus, even if it did not have spikes, it still would have been hard for *Ankylosaurus* to be overturned.) Also, if it wanted to, this plant eater could even strike an attacker with its heavy, club-like tail.

Marine Reptiles

While dinosaurs roamed the lands, there were many other reptiles that lived in the oceans, lakes, and rivers of the world. These reptiles ranged in size from only a few inches long to creatures that reached over 70 feet long. Some had long, slender necks and sharp teeth. Others had short, stocky necks with long jaws. These reptiles were not di-nosaurs, since the definition of a dinosaur states that it is an animal that lived only on land. But these animals were similar to di-nosaurs because they were reptiles and not fish or mammals. Let's take a look at some of the most common water-living reptiles.

Ichthyosaurs

One of the most common and interesting categories of marine reptiles is the ichthyosaurs. The name ichthyosaur means "fish lizard" or "fish reptile." After looking at this "fish lizard," it is not difficult to see why it was given such a name. Although ichthyosaurs look like fish or dolphins, most scientists think they were actually reptiles.

Ichthyosaurs came in all shapes and sizes. They could be only a few feet long, or they could grow to almost 70 feet long. Of course, their weight depended on their size. Some weighed only a few hundred pounds, while others weighed several tons. The huge eyes

Plesiosaurs

Another group of well-known marine reptiles is the plesiosaurs. The name plesiosaur means "near-lizard." These creatures had flippers like the ichthyosaurs, but they did not look as much like fish or dolphins. Plesiosaurs are divided into two groups. The creatures in the first group had a small head attached to a long neck that looked like a snake connected to a thick, wide body. The other group of plesiosaurs had short, thick necks and long heads with strong jaws.

Elasmosaurus is an example of a plesiosaur with a long, snake-like neck. *Elasmosaurus* means "thin-plated lizard." This water dweller could grow to be about 46 feet long. Its neck was about 26 feet long—over half of its total length—and it alone had about 70 vertebrae (spinal bones). Compare that to a human's neck, which has only 7-8 vertebrae, and you begin to see just how long this creature's neck really was. Fossils of *Elasmosaurus* show us that its head was small, but its mouth had many sharp teeth. It probably ate other marine reptiles, fish, and squid. Its four, paddle-like flippers made it an excellent swimmer. Like the other marine reptiles, this creature was not a dinosaur.

of ichthyosaurs were their most distinctive feature. In fact, an ichthyosaur had eyes that were probably the largest in proportion to its body of any animal to ever live. These huge eyes would have helped the ichthyosaurs find smaller fish and squid-like animals to eat. One of the most common ichthyosaurs was *Ichthyosaurus*. The term ichthyo**saurs** deals with a large group of different animals that varied in size and shape, while the term *Ichthyosaurus* deals with one specific animal in the group.

Ichthyosaurus grew to be about 6½ feet long and weighed about 200 pounds. With its large eyes and massive ear bones, this creature probably had keen eyesight and a wonderful sense of hearing. Also, the strong flippers and sleek tail would have made it an excellent swimmer. Scientists have estimated that it could swim 25 miles per hour. Paleontologists have discovered hundreds of *Ichthyosaurus* fossils in countries such as Canada, England, Germany, and Greenland.

Kronosaurus is an example of the second type of plesiosaur that had a short, stocky neck with a large head. This huge creature (which can be seen on pages 38 and 39) reigned as one of the most terrible predators of the oceans. It could reach lengths of over 30 feet, with a head 6-10 feet long (its head was almost one-third of its entire length). With powerful jaws and a mouth full of sharp teeth, the *Kronosaurus* could have eaten just about anything in the sea. In the back of its jaw, it had large, round teeth that some scientists believe were used to crack shelled animals. Inside the stomach cavities of fossilized *Kronosaurs*, scientists have found pieces of turtles and other plesiosaurs. Needless to say, you would not want to swim in waters with this beast.

In the book of Job, chapter 41, we read about an ancient water-dwelling creature called leviathan. The leviathan had "terrible teeth all around" its mouth, and it had scales and sharp undersides. We do not know exactly what leviathan was, but after looking at some fossils of interesting creatures like *Elasmosaurus* and *Kronosaurus*, we can see that amazing animals such as the leviathan did once exist.

The Mixosaurus *(shown above) and the* Peloneustes *(shown below) were other marine reptiles that once inhabited the oceans and seas.*

FLYING REPTILES

We know that nearly all birds can fly. Many kinds of insects can fly. Even mammals, such as the bat, can soar through the air. But reptiles? Who has ever heard of a flying reptile? Aren't all reptiles "ground bound?" Some people may be surprised to learn that flying birds, insects, and mammals once shared the sky with flying reptiles. (The largest flying reptile in this picture is the *Quetzalcoatlus*.)

EVIDENCE THAT HUMANS LIVED WITH DINOSAURS

An Ancient Picture of a Dinosaur

Suppose your teacher asked you to take out a pencil and paper and draw a Kabolib. What would you draw? You probably wouldn't draw anything because you don't know what a Kabolib is and you certainly don't know what one looks like. The truth is, there is no Kabolib; it is a made-up word that has no meaning. But we can learn from this word that in order to draw something a person must see it or have it described.

In the country of Cambodia, an ancient emperor named Jayavarman VII built a temple to honor his mother. He finished building the temple in A.D. 1186. Beautiful stone statues and carvings decorate the walls and columns of the temple. In the middle of all these beautiful carvings, there is a row of animals carved on a pillar. Most of the animals are not unusual—a monkey, a deer, some parrots. But one of the animals is very interesting because it looks like a *Stegosaurus*!

Why is a carving of a *Stegosaurus* so interesting? Evolutionary scientists say that dinosaurs died out about 60 million years ago. They say that humans could not have seen living dinosaurs. But the carving on the Cambodian temple proves that idea is false. How would the person carving the temple almost a thousand years ago have known what a *Stegosaurus* looked like unless he had seen one, or someone had described it to him?

Today we know what dinosaurs looked like because people spend millions of dollars digging up their bones. But this digging did not start in modern times until about 1822—more than 600 years after the temple was built. The very best explanation is that whoever carved the temple had seen a *Stegosaurus*. That idea might sound strange to a person who believes in evolution, but not to someone who has read the Bible. The Bible says that God made everything in six days. He made humans on day six, along with all land-living animals. Since dinosaurs were land-living animals, they were made on day six of Creation, along with humans. The fact that humans saw dinosaurs fits perfectly with what the Bible says.

Stegosaurus *image courtesy of www.Bible.ca*

Natural Bridges National Monument Petroglyph

Natural Bridges National Monument is located in a barren part of southeastern Utah. On the underside of its second largest bridge (Kachina Bridge), several petroglyphs (rock carvings) and pictographs (rock paintings) exist, which rock-art experts believe to be anywhere from 500 to 1,500 years old. The carvings are thought to be the work of the Anasazi Indians who once lived in that area of southeastern Utah. A mountain goat, a human figure, multiple hand prints, and many other carvings and drawings are seen easily underneath the bridge on both sides of the span. The most fascinating piece of rock art at Kachina Bridge, however, is the petroglyph that looks exactly like a dinosaur. This figure, which is carved into the rock, has a long, thick tail, a long neck, a wide midsection, and a small head. Any unbiased visitor to Kachina Bridge would have to admit that this particular petroglyph looks like a dinosaur—specifically an *Apatosaurus* (more popularly known as *Brontosaurus*). But is it really genuine? Two well-known rock-art experts have written about this particular petroglyph, and neither has suggested that it is a modern-day fake. One of these rock-art experts is a man named

a man named Francis Barnes—an evolutionist who is widely known for his knowledge on rock art of the American Southwest. He stated: "There is a petroglyph in Natural Bridges National Monument that bears a startling resemblance to a dinosaur, specifically a *Brontosaurus*, with long tail and neck,

To help you see the image, we have enhanced the color of certain portions and circled both the human figure in the upper left-hand section and the dinosaur figure to the right.

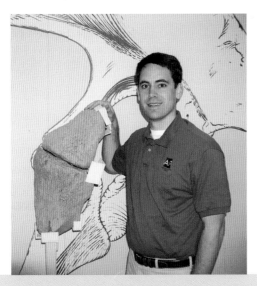

About 45 miles from the dinosaur petroglyph, The Dinosaur Museum in Blanding, Utah has a section of an Apatosaurus *hip fossil on display that was found near the area. This find shows that the dinosaur was in the area, and could have been seen by early Indians.*

small head and all." The other evolutionary rock-art specialist, Dennis Slifer, made this statement about the same petroglyph: "One of the most curious designs is a petroglyph that resembles a dinosaur."

Truly, the dinosaur petroglyph at Natural Bridges National Monument shows every sign of being an actual drawing of a real dinosaur by a people who lived in that area of Utah hundreds or perhaps even 1,000 years before the first dinosaur fossil was found in modern times (1820s). The best way to explain this drawing is to admit that people have seen dinosaurs in the past. Interestingly, about 45 miles away from the carving, bones of an *Apatosaurus* were discovered, and currently are on display at The Dinosaur Museum in Blanding, Utah.

51

Dinosaur Figurines in Mexico

In 1945, a German businessman by the name of Waldemar Julsrud was riding a horse near the foot of the El Toro mountain in Acambaro, Mexico. Looking at the ground, he noticed some carved stone and ceramic pieces sticking up, half buried in the dirt. He jumped off his horse and began to dig up the artifacts, which were unlike any he had ever seen. He was familiar with many artifacts from the ancient Indian tribes that had lived in the area, but these looked even older. Thinking that there might be more of the ceramics and stone carvings, he made a deal with a local farmer.

musical instruments, masks, idols, and other such things. Each one was different from the others, since they were not made using a mold, but were handcrafted. Among the figurines, hundreds of dinosaur sculptures were found. Some of the dinosaur sculptures were as much as five feet long. Among the different dinosaur figurines found,

dinosaurs such as the *Triceratops, Stegosaurus, Iguanodon, Brachiosaurus,* and *Tyrannosaurus rex* could be identified.

For every unbroken piece the farmer dug up, Julsrud would pay him 1 peso (about 12 cents). In all, about 20,000 artifacts were found. Many of them were faces of people,

Many people did not believe that the figurines could be really old, because they were such accurate models of the dinosaurs. Since dinosaurs and man are thought to have been separated by millions of years, many scien-

tists who believe in evolution suggested that the figurines were fakes. But it is impossible for them to be fake, because other people since the 1940s have found the same type of figurines. In fact, in order to prove that the artifacts were not faked, a man named Charles Hapgood found a house that had been built in the 1930s, 14 years before dinosaur figurines were found. Beneath the concrete living room floor, Hapgood found exactly what he expected to find—more figurines. He proved that Julsrud could not have faked the discovery.

Since the 1940s, over 33,000 figurines have been found. Hundreds of them are accurate models of dinosaurs. Several scientists have investigated the figurines, eyewitnesses have seen them dug out of the ground, and dating has been done that suggests they are very old. How could the people at Acambaro have known what dinosaurs looked like if they had not seen them? The truth is, dinosaurs and man lived together in the past. God created all the animals, and Adam and Eve, on days five and six of the Creation week. Dinosaurs and humans have never been separated by millions of years, and the Acambaro figurines help prove this beyond any doubt.

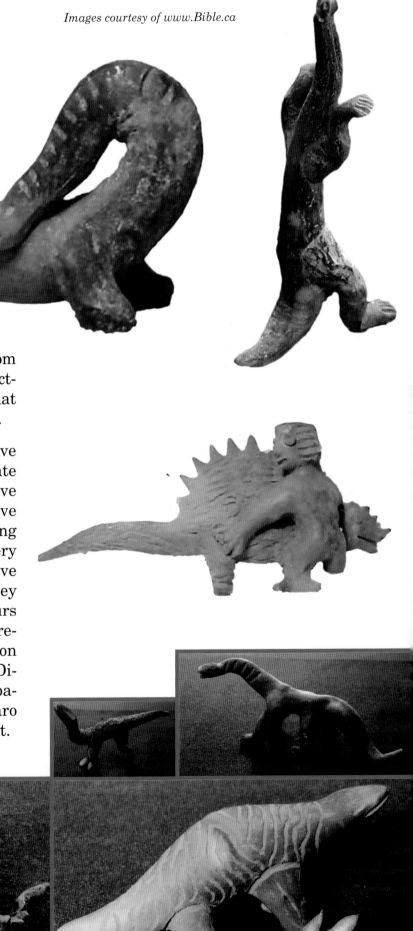

Samuel Hubbard and the Rock Drawing

In the fall of 1924, Samuel Hubbard and Charles Gilmore went on a hunt. They were not hunting animals or dinosaurs. They were hunting ancient artifacts that they thought would prove Indians once lived near the Grand Canyon. Samuel Hubbard had been to the site many years earlier in 1894 and had seen some strange artifacts. He had tried to convince other scientists of their importance, but few were willing to listen. Finally, he arranged for Charles Gilmore to go with him. Dr. Gilmore was a respected scientist working with the United States National Museum. They needed money to pay for their trip, so they asked a rich man named E.L. Doheny to support them. He agreed to finance their mission, which was called "the Doheny Expedition." When the men arrived

at the Havai Supai Canyon, they began looking for the artifacts that Hubbard had seen years before. The artifacts were still there, just as Hubbard had remembered. On the canyon wall, the men found rock carvings (known as petroglyphs) of different animals: an ibex (wild goat), an elephant, and —a dinosaur. Samuel Hubbard wrote that the dinosaur stood upright in a feeding or a fighting position. He also said: "The fact that the animal is upright and balanced on its tail would seem to indicate that the prehistoric artist must have seen it alive." How could ancient people have carved such an accurate picture of a dinosaur on the canyon wall if they had never seen a dinosaur, or if they had never talked to someone who had seen a dinosaur and who could describe it to them?

Not only did they find the petroglyph of a creature that looked like a dinosaur, but the men also found several dinosaur footprints. Mr. Hubbard said this about the footprints: "That dinosaurs were in the vicinity, is proved by the tracks we discovered, which were identified by Mr. Gilmore as belonging to one of the carnivorous dinosaurs." The men of the Doheny Expedition took photo-

Courtesy of www.Bible.ca

graphs of the drawings and documented the details of their trip. Very few scientists today who believe in evolution want to talk about the Doheny Expedition because the pictures taken by a respected scientist show that humans and dinosaurs lived at the same time.

Courtesy of Eden Communications

EDMONTOSAURUS

22,000 pounds, and could easily crush a man just by stepping on him. Yet, for thousands of years humans have been known to live with, and tame, these creatures. Over 2,200 years ago, the empire of Carthage used tamed African elephants (the largest elephants in the world) to battle the Romans. Today, many elephants are still being controlled by man. Tamed elephants are used in various Asian countries to perform in religious ceremonies, or to do physical labor like hauling lumber or transporting people from place to place. Tamed elephants are also frequently seen performing at circuses.

Humans have been able to live alongside elephants for thousands of years. Some humans and elephants even have become good "friends." So why is it so hard for people to think of humans living next to some of the large dinosaurs? Yes, some dinosaurs like *Brachiosaurus* grew to be about four times larger than the largest elephants. But, if man can work with, play, and go to battle alongside (or on top of) elephants—the largest land animals on Earth today—it surely is not absurd to think humans did similar things with certain dinosaurs.

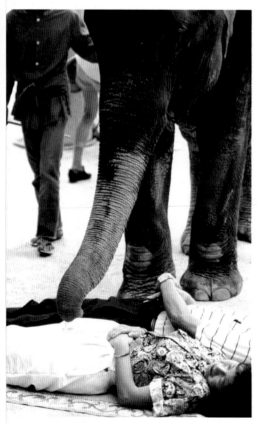

Whales are the largest animals that have ever existed on Earth—larger than any elephant or dinosaur. Blue whales have been known

to weigh as much as 400,000 pounds, have a heart the size of a small car, and a tongue large enough to hold 50 people. Yet, humans have hunted many species of whales for centuries. Some people today ride in small boats or swim next to some of these massive creatures.

Killer whales are another one of God's magnificent creatures that live with us on this Earth. Killer whales are one of the oceans' fiercest predators, and are able to kill much larger whales when swimming in packs (known as "pods"). Killer whales hunt so well that very few animals can escape from them. Kill-

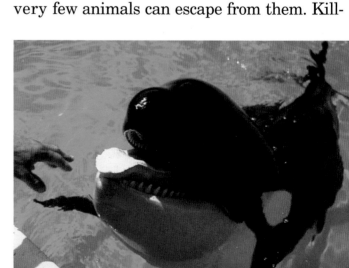

58

er whales eat thousands of pounds of mammal meat every year. Seals, sea lions, walruses, otters, polar bears, and even a moose have all been found in the stomachs of these vicious creatures.

Amazingly, these large "killing machines" (weighing as much as 10,000 pounds) can be captured, tamed, and trained to do all sorts of things. The famous orcas living at Sea World in Orlando, Florida occasionally take their trainers for rides on their backs. Trainers of killer whales have even been known to stick their heads inside the whales' mouths (which usually hold about 40-56 large, 3-inch-long teeth) without getting bitten.

How can a 150-pound man teach a 10,000-pound whale how to jump over hurdles, ring bells, and perform other neat tricks without being harmed? The answer is found (at least partly) in Genesis 1:27-28:

> So God created man in His own image; in the image of God He created him; male and female He created them. Then God blessed them, and God said to them,

"Be fruitful and multiply; fill the earth and **subdue** it; have **dominion** over the fish of the sea, over the birds of the air, and over every living thing that moves on the earth."

The reason man can tame even the largest and most vicious creatures on Earth is because God created man higher than animals, and gave him the ability to "subdue" them and have "dominion" over them.

If man can live with and tame such amazing creatures as the elephant, the blue whale, and the killer whale, as well as lions, tigers, and bears, it should not be hard to understand that man could have lived with, and possibly even tamed, the dinosaurs.

IT COULDN'T LAST THAT LONG

What happens to a chicken bone that gets left outside in the yard? Most of the time a dog or cat eats it or buries it in the ground. But what would happen if it were buried very quickly? It might turn into a chicken-bone fossil. A fossil is something that is left by a plant, animal, or person. As we said earlier, when a fossil forms, the bone and "stuff" inside the bone (like bone marrow or blood cells) are replaced by minerals that are hard like rock. The minerals form in the exact shape of the bone. So, if our chicken bone fossilized, we would dig up a very hard, rocky replica of our bone.

This process sometimes occurred with dinosaur bones. They are buried in the ground

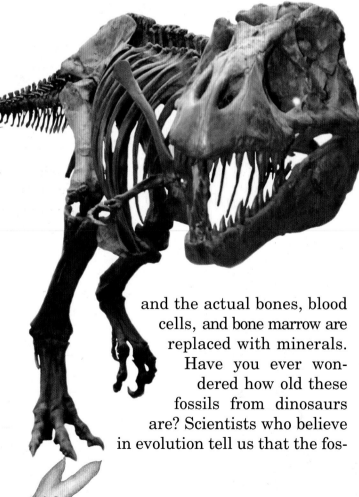

and the actual bones, blood cells, and bone marrow are replaced with minerals. Have you ever wondered how old these fossils from dinosaurs are? Scientists who believe in evolution tell us that the fos-

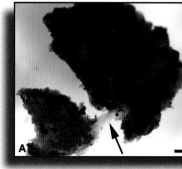

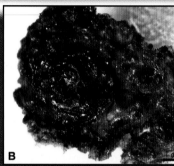

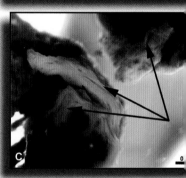

sils from dinosaurs are over 60 million years old. But that simply is not true.

Recently, something happened that helps disprove the idea that dinosaur bones are millions of years old. Scientists uncovered a fossil from a *Tyrannosaurus rex*. But when they broke the fossil open, it still had soft tissues. They had not been replaced by rocky minerals. We know that soft tissue could not last millions of years buried underground. It would have decayed or been fossilized.

Associated Press Copyright 20

Evolutionary scientists should admit that they are wrong. They should admit that dinosaur bones are not millions of years old. But that is not what they have done. Instead, they have said that the soft tissue somehow lasted 65 million years. But that cannot be true. An honest person who found soft tissue in a dinosaur fossil would admit that the fossil could not be millions of years old. This find helps us to see that dinosaurs did not live millions of years ago, but were created by God only a few thousand years ago, during the Creation week we read about in Genesis 1.

Life in Layers

Did you know that if you could look at the Earth in a jar, you would see layers? Scientists call these layers the geologic column. Geology is the study of the Earth, which is why these layers are called the geologic column.

In these layers of the Earth, we find millions of different fossils. Evolutionists teach that the "simplest" organisms are found in the "oldest" layers at the bottom of the geologic column, while more "complex" organisms are located in "younger" layers at the top. Evolutionists also teach that each layer was laid down over millions of years, and that the fossils found in the layers represent plants and animals that evolved during that time.

But neither of these teachings is true. In fact, the idea that these layers were laid down over long periods of time, that they contain organisms in a "simple-to-complex" order, and that they somehow "prove" evolution, has many serious problems. For example, some plant and animal fossils cut through several layers. Does that mean that these plants or animals were being fossilized over millions of years? Also, those animals that look "simple" aren't as simple as people once thought. Trilobites (sea-living animals with a shell, found in the lower layers of the column) had more complex eyes than most of the "complex" animals found above them. How could they be progressing from "simple to complex" if the ones on the bottom were already complex?

Another problem with the idea of long ages of time has to do with the Flood of Noah. Imagine pouring layers of different-colored sand into a jar. Then imagine dumping water into that jar very quickly and shaking it up really hard. When it settled out, would the bottom layer of sand be the one you poured in first? No! Some of the colors you poured in last would mix with those you put in first, making it impossible to know which sand was poured in first. Those who look at the geologic column and say it took millions of years to form do not even consider the great Flood of Noah.

When we examine the geologic column more closely, we find that it gives some good evidence for Creation. For example, if evolution were true, then we would expect to see many half-and-half fossils (such as a half-reptile/half-mammal) gradually changing from one kind of animal into another. But what we really find are millions of animals and plants that are fully formed, and that appear in the column with no gradual line of fossils before them—which is exactly what you would expect to find in a world that was created!

Earth's Extraordinary Evidence!

Have you ever had someone tell you something, and then later you found out that what you had been told wasn't true? It's sad, but sometimes people tell us things that simply aren't right. Perhaps this is why the Bible commands us to "test all things; hold fast what is good" (1 Thessalonians 5:21). That's good advice, especially when people tell us things that clearly contradict God's Word.

Many of us have been taught that the geologic column "proves" that evolution is true and that the Earth is old. As you get older, various people may tell you this is true, but it's not. Actually, the geologic column provides extraordinary evidence which shows that evolution is **not** true and that the Earth is **not** ancient. Consider the following.

TREE TRUNK POLYSTRATE FOSSILS

Embedded in rocks all over the globe are "polystrate" fossils. Polystrate means "many layers" and refers to fossils that cut through at least two layers of the geologic column. For example, geologists have discovered tree trunks buried vertically (up and down) through two, three, four, or more sections of rock—rock that evolutionists suggest was deposited over millions of years. In Nova Scotia, there are many upright fossil trees scattered throughout layers extending upward more than 2,500 feet. However, organic material (like wood) that is exposed to the elements will rot, not fossilize. Scientists have had to admit that the trees must have been preserved very quickly.

Courtesy of www.Bible.ca

62

THE WHALE POLYSTRATE FOSSIL

Geologists also have discovered polystrate animal fossils. One of the most famous is the fossilized skeleton of a whale discovered in 1976 near Lompoc, California. The whale is covered in "diatomaceous [die-uh-toe-MAY-shus] earth." Diatoms are microscopic algae. As diatoms die, their skeletons form deposits—a process that evolutionists say is extremely slow. But the whale (with a skull more than 7 feet thick) is completely covered by the diatomaceous earth. There is simply no way the whale could have remained on its back for hundreds of years while diatoms covered it, because it would have decayed or been eaten by scavengers. It is clear from this extraordinary evidence that the long ages attached to the geologic column simply are not correct.

FOSSILIZED FOOTPRINT & TRILOBITE

In 1968, a man in Utah named William Meister discovered a fossilized footprint of a human wearing a sandal. Inside the print was a trilobite (a marine organism). Evolutionists teach that trilobites became extinct 500 million years before man appeared, but the Earth's extraordinary evidence from the geologic column shows us that evolutionists are wrong. [The Bible also teaches us that such an idea is wrong, since God created all things in six days (Exodus 20:11).]

There are many other examples from the geologic column which show that evolution isn't true and the Earth isn't old. Remember: "Test all things; hold fast what is good." When people tell you something that disagrees with God's Word, don't believe it. "Test it" against the actual evidence, and then you will know the real truth of the matter.

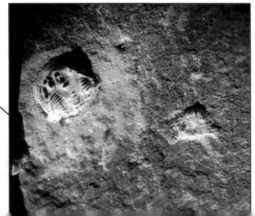

Images courtesy of the Creation Evidence Museum

63

A Living "Dinosaur"

For decades, evolutionists taught that coelacanths (SEE-luh-kanths) became extinct about the same time dinosaurs did (supposedly 65 million years ago). In the past, it was said that these fish gradually developed legs and began to live on land and then, sometime later, became extinct. Evolutionists thought that these fish were "the missing link" between water and land animals. Similar to the ape-like creatures that allegedly evolved into humans, these fish were said to have evolved into land animals millions of years ago. In fact, evolutionary scientists used the coelacanth as a part of their "index fossil" system, meaning that any rocks that contained coelacanth fossils were considered to be at least 65 million years old (with other fossils in those rocks assumed to be at least that old as well).

Until 1938, evolutionists believed that men and coelacanths could not possibly have lived at the same time. These creatures were known only from the fossils that evolutionists claimed were millions of years old. But then, on December 24, 1938, the scientific world was "rocked" when an unidentified fish five feet long and weighing over 100 pounds was brought to shore in South Africa. It was caught in the Indian Ocean near Madagascar. The fisherman who netted the fish (having no idea what the creature's proper name was) called it "the great sea lizard" because its pectoral fins looked more like little fringed legs. Once scientists examined this strange creature, however, they confirmed what formerly was thought impossible—a coelacanth had been caught in modern times! One evolutionist said that

he could not have been more surprised if he had come across **a living dinosaur**. After all, according to their theory, coelacanths evolved before dinosaurs and became extinct at about the same time dinosaurs did.

Since 1938, over 100 coelacanths have been caught. In 1952, they were seen swimming near the Comoro Islands in the Indian Ocean. Another population was found in 1998 off the coast of Indonesia. Surprisingly, local Indonesian fishermen were quite familiar with this fish, having caught them for years, though scientists were totally unaware they lived in that region.

Modern-day coelacanths look exactly like their fossil counterparts (which are mistakenly dated as being millions of years old). The fact that these modern-day creatures have stayed the same as their fossilized ancestors is no surprise to Christians. The Bible teaches that animals produce "after their kind" (Genesis 1:21,24), and **the fossil record proves that this is exactly what has happened.** Fish never gradually developed over millions of years into land animals any more than ape-like creatures developed into humans.

What makes the evolutionary idea about coelacanths being a missing link even more outrageous is that these fish live near the ocean floor. Scientists now know that the coelacanth is a deep-water fish that rarely approaches within less than 500 feet of the surface. So, even if there was a missing link between fish and land animals (and you can be sure that there was not), since these fish hardly ever swim near the water surface (and close to land), they could not have been the missing link.

In reality, coelacanths have always been coelacanths—nothing more and nothing less. Their discovery in modern times makes a mockery of evolutionary dating methods and takes us back to the time of the dinosaur, which was not all that long ago.

Dinosaurs and the Bible

If you have ever read through the Bible in search for the word "dinosaur," you may have noticed that this word is missing. Not one time is the word "dinosaur" mentioned in all of God's Word. But does that mean that the Bible has nothing to say about these wonderful creatures? No. You see, just because the Bible does not mention the actual word "dinosaur," that does not mean that it never mentions the animals we know as dinosaurs.

First of all, the Bible discusses dinosaurs in the same books, chapters, and verses that speak of kangaroos, anteaters, and platypuses. Where is that? In Exodus 20:11, the Bible states: "For in six days the Lord made the heavens and the earth, the sea, **and all that is in them**, and rested the seventh day." In Genesis 1:20-27, we learn that God made **all living** creatures on days five and six of the Creation week. While these verses do not mention dinosaurs **by name**, it is clear that God created all types of animals within the six days of Creation—including dinosaurs. Genesis 2:1 informs us that at the end of day six, God was finished with His creation. If God created everything in six days and did not create anything else after those six days, then dinosaurs must have been a part of that six-day Creation. And so, just as we know that God created kangaroos, anteaters, and platypuses (even though the Bible never mentions them specifically by name), we can know that God created the dinosaurs during the Creation week.

BEHEMOTH

Something else to consider is that there is a creature described by God in Job chapter 40 that sounds exactly like a dinosaur. While God was having a discussion with Job, He asked Job if he had seen the "behemoth" [buh-HE-moth]? God described the animal by saying:

> He eats grass like an ox. See now, his strength is in his hips, and his power is in his stomach muscles. He moves his tail like a cedar; the sinews [tendons] of his thighs are tightly knit. His bones are like beams of bronze, his ribs like bars of iron. He is the first [chief] of the ways of God; only He who made him can bring near His sword (Job 40:15-19).

Certainly, no other creature (living or extinct) fits this description better than a dinosaur. Many dinosaurs had huge tails "like a cedar" tree. Their bones were like "beams of bronze." Their ribs were like "bars of iron." And they easily could be called the "chief of the ways of God." (Certain dinosaurs were the largest land-living animals ever to roam the Earth!)

Some have argued that the creature God described in Job 40 was a hippopotamus. While it is true that a few similarities do exist between the behemoth and the hippo, some of the details simply do not fit. God described the behemoth as a creature that "moves his tail like a cedar" (40:17), yet the tail of the hippo is short and small like that of a pig, and is a mere twig in comparison with a cedar.

[NOTE: Throughout Scripture, "cedars" were known for their great length (read Isaiah 37:24 and Ezekiel 31:3).] The behemoth is said to be "chief of the ways of God" (40: 19). Surely this would rule out the hippo, since at full size it is but 7 feet high and weighs about 7,000 pounds. And even though the

elephant is twice the size of a hippo, even it was small compared to the 150,000-pound dinosaurs that once walked the Earth. The truth is, there is not an animal on Earth today that comes close to fitting this description of behemoth.

LEVIATHAN

In the book of Job, we also can read of another creature that sounds very similar to a dinosaur-like, water-living reptile. God described this beast in Job chapter 41.

- You can't catch him with a hook (vss. 1-2).

- You can't kill him with a spear (vs. 26).

- He laughs at the threat of javelins (vs. 29).

- When he raises himself up, the mighty are afraid (vss. 25,34).

- When he swims, the water boils with commotion (vss. 31-32).

- His underside is like sharp pieces of broken pottery that leave pointed marks in the mud (vs. 30).

- Flashes of light and smoke expel from his nostrils like steam coming out of a boiling pot (vss. 18,20).

- Sparks of fire shoot out of his mouth, and his eyes glow like the morning sun (vss. 18-19,21).

- He is too powerful and ferocious to be captured by man (vss. 9-10,33).

What is this amazing creature that God described in His conversation with Job? It is called leviathan (luh-VIE-uh-thun) in verse one. But what is a leviathan? Some suggest that the leviathan was a crocodile. Others believe that it was a whale. However, the description of leviathan does not fit either of these two animals. In fact, the description of this creature does not fit that of any known animal present in the world today. Thus, it must be some type of extinct creature. But

what kind? God's description of leviathan is similar to the descriptions we have of dinosaur-like, water-living reptiles that once terrorized the waters—not millions of years ago as some believe, but only a few thousand years ago when Job was alive.

Is it possible that in Job's day there was a dinosaur-like, water-living reptile called leviathan that exhaled fire and smoke? Some think that leviathan was just imaginary, but God was not talking to Job about make-believe, mythological creatures. In the chapters just before His descriptions of leviathan and behemoth, God asked Job about real animals like the wild donkey and the wild ox, as well as mountain goats, horses, lions, and hawks. Leviathan and behemoth were included along with **real** creatures that Job knew about. He even spoke of the behemoth as being "made along with" Job (40:15).

Other Amazing Creatures

Although many have said that God never created such animals as the behemoth of Job 40 or the leviathan of Job 41, when you stop and consider some of God's other amazing creatures, it is not difficult to accept that a dragon-like creature (called leviathan) once lived upon the Earth.

The Electric Eel

The electric eel can pack an electrical punch greater than the shock that you would get from sticking your finger into an electrical socket. The electricity from this amazing creature arises from a group of highly compacted nerve endings found all along its body. Each one of these nerve endings has a small electric voltage that, when added together, can be a shocking experience! A full-grown eel can produce enough electricity—600 volts—to stun a horse. Eels use this electrical current as self-defense and a way to stun their prey. Yet, they live in water, don't shock themselves, and can recharge without an extension cord.

The Lightning Bug

Lightning bugs (also called fireflies) are little beetles that carry their own "flashlights." These insects have a special chemical called luciferin (lew-SIF-er-in), which they store in their abdomens. When this chemical comes into contact with oxygen from air they breathe, fireflies give off a bright flash of light. The whole process is called bioluminescence (by-oh-LOO-meh-NES-sense). According to scientists, this light helps fireflies find their mates. The male flashes his light first, and when the female sees it, she flashes her light. This tells the male where she is. What an incredible way to find a mate!

70

THE BOMBARDIER BEETLE

Perhaps one of the most amazing animals on Earth today is a little insect known as the bombardier beetle. This bug packs a powerful, explosive defense mechanism. Inside its body, it has tiny glands that secrete two chemicals into a "storage tank" (known as a "collecting vesicle"). Those chemicals are hydrogen peroxide and hydroquinones (hi-dro-kwi-NŌNS).

If an enemy attacks the beetle, it empties these two chemicals into a special "explosion chamber." Then it adds special enzymes to the mixture. As a result, the chemicals form a solution that reaches the boiling point of water (100° Celsius or 212° Fahrenheit) in just a couple of seconds. The beetle can then take aim with two small gun-like projections on the rear of its body and fire the boiling mixture into the face of its attacker. What a remarkable creature!

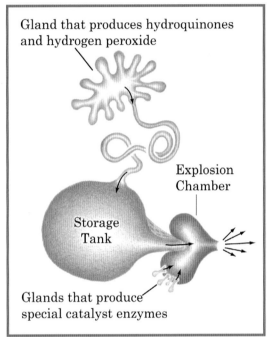

Gland that produces hydroquinones and hydrogen peroxide

Explosion Chamber

Storage Tank

Glands that produce special catalyst enzymes

When you realize that God has created a beetle that produces explosive chemical reactions, a bug that can produce "light," and eels that produce electricity, it is not difficult to accept the fact that there once lived a creature that shot sparks of fire out of its mouth and expelled smoke from its nostrils.

Artwork on this and facing page by Thomas A. Tarpley

Picture used with permission from Dr. Thomas Eisner

71

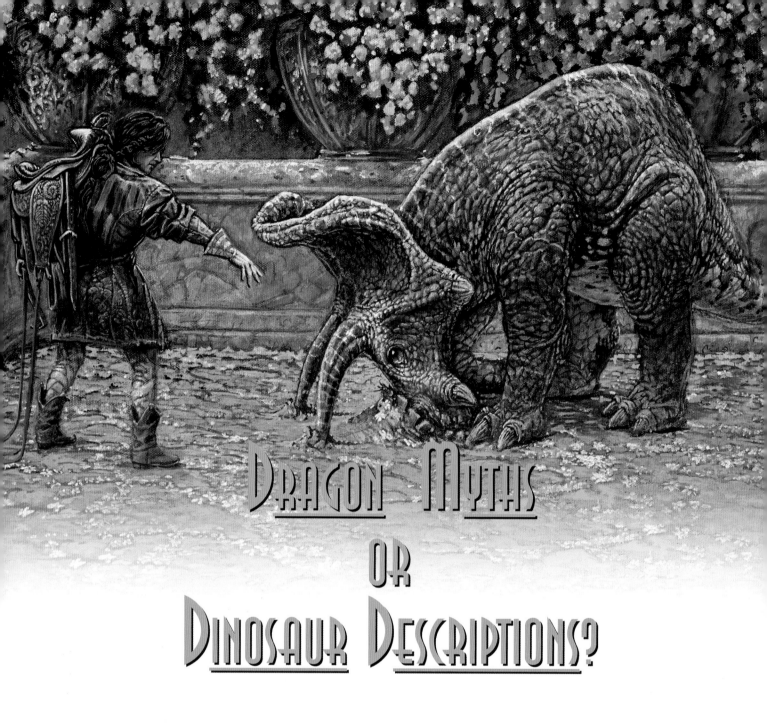

Dragon Myths

or

Dinosaur Descriptions?

If dinosaurs and humans once walked the Earth together (as the Bible clearly teaches they did—read Exodus 20:11), it is logical to conclude that humans would have left behind at least two different types of evidence to show they had lived with dinosaurs. First, similar to how we take pictures of places we visit and wildlife we see in modern times, those living hundreds or thousands of years ago would likely have drawn or carved pictures of dinosaurs, as well as many other an-

imals. (Indeed, we have seen that is exactly what they did.) Second, just as we tell stories today of things that we have seen and heard, ancient people would also have told stories about dinosaurs, if they ever encountered these creatures. Do such stories exist? They certainly do.

A wide variety of stories of large reptiles have been passed down from cultures all over the world. Many of these creatures

sound very much like dinosaurs, or dinosaur-like (marine or flying) reptiles. However, they are not called dinosaurs in these stories, but dragons. Since the term dinosaur (meaning "fearfully great reptile") was not coined until the early 1840s, stories told previously of "fearfully great reptiles" would not have included the word dinosaur. Instead, the name attached to these creatures was "dragon."

Stories about dragons were around long before we learned about dinosaurs in modern times from the fossil record. One evolutionist wrote: "Dragon legends have been with humanity since the dawn of recorded history"— thousands of years ago. The Chinese told of one ancient emperor who raised a dragon in his palace. In the 1200s, Italian explorer Marco Polo wrote of seeing long, two-legged reptiles (called "lindworms") while passing through central Asia.

In A.D. 1450, Englishmen reported seeing two huge reptiles fighting on the banks of the river Stour. Around A.D. 1405, in Bures, United Kingdom, townsmen told of

seeing "a dragon, vast in body, with a crested head, teeth like a saw, and a tail, extending to an enormous length." Wales, whose national flag boldly displays a red dragon (an animal associated with the country for centuries), reportedly once had many dinosaur-like, flying reptiles occupying its airspace. They were called "winged serpents" and described as having colorful "crests" on their heads.

The ancient Babylonians told about a four-legged, scaly, powerful creature with a long neck,

73

a horned head, a lengthy tail, and a snake-like tongue. This animal, which they called sirrush, is even depicted on a gate discovered in 1899 next to two real animals: a lion and a bull. Many people believe that sirrush also was a real animal.

Have some dragon legends been exaggerated over time? Of course. Just as people today tend to embellish the size of a fish they have caught or the size of a dog that nips their leg, people in the past said some things about dragons that may not be true. But such inaccuracies do not mean dragons never lived.

Any honest person who reads the various dragon legends must admit that the creatures in these stories normally do not sound like animals currently living on Earth. Large reptiles with long necks, scaly skin, horned heads, four legs, and lengthy tails sound like dinosaurs. Dragon legends about flying snake-like reptiles with two legs, large wingspans, slender tails, and toothed beaks sound much more like the dinosaur-like, flying reptiles of the past (*Quetzalcoatlus*, *Rhamphorhynchus*, and *Pterodactyl*) than any animal alive today. Even the stories of massive, powerful sea reptiles, at least one of which breathed fire (read Job 41:18-21), sound very much like some of the dinosaur-like, marine reptiles of the past.

In 2003, a nearly complete dinosaur skull was excavated in South Dakota. The long, knobby, spiky skull appeared so similar to

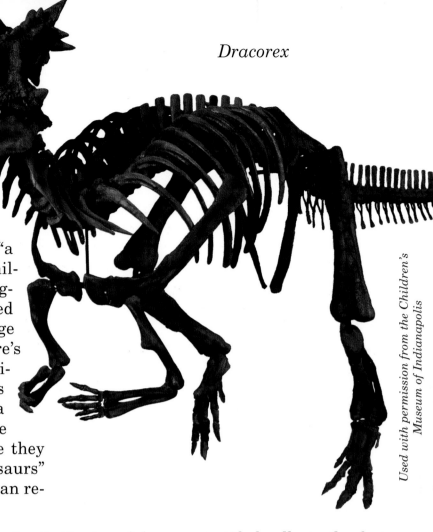

Dracorex

descriptions and paintings of certain "legendary" dragons, it actually was named *Dracorex*, meaning "dragon king." The Children's Museum of Indianapolis, which now possesses the skull, referred to it as "a new type of dinosaur" that is "66-million-years-old" and "looks like a dragon." The Children's Museum displayed a placard next to a *Dracorex* image that read: "When we saw this creature's head, we weren't sure what kind of dinosaur it was. Its spiky horns, bumps and long muzzle looked more like a dragon." A dinosaur that looks more like a dragon? Maybe that's because they were dragons! "Dragons" and "dinosaurs" are simply two different words that can refer to the same creature.

What good reason exists for the hundreds of dragon legends all around the world? Why did people in different places and times, separated by thousands of miles, all come up with stories of giant reptiles that sound more like extinct dinosaurs than any other animal on Earth? The reasonable answer is: humans and dinosaurs once lived together, and stories of their interaction were passed down from generation to generation. Evolutionists, however, must continue to reject the obvious in order to believe that dinosaurs became extinct 65 million years before humans were present on Earth.

Stories of dragons testify loudly to the fact that dinosaurs and humans once lived together. Truly, evolutionists cannot logically explain away these "dinosaur descriptions."

WHERE DID THE DINOSAURS GO?

It seems that no one wants to know why the saber-toothed tiger became extinct. And rarely do people question why the woolly mammoth died out. But everyone wants to know what happened to the dinosaurs.

Why are dinosaurs no longer on the Earth? What drove them into extinction? The truth is, no one knows why the dinosaurs died out, although many people who believe in evolution have suggested a number of reasons.

Some believe that small, rat-like mammals evolved and ate all of the dinosaur eggs until none was left. Others think that a terrible disease struck the dinosaurs, resulting in worldwide extinction. Some scientists say that the oxygen levels in the air were much higher when the dinosaurs lived than they are now. As the oxygen levels decreased over time to current levels, dinosaurs found it harder and harder to breathe and eventually became extinct.

The most widely accepted theory is that an asteroid the size of a large city (about six miles in diameter) smashed into the Earth, throwing tons of dust into the air. This dust was then carried around the planet by jet stream winds, and it soon stopped many of the Sun's rays from reaching the ground. Without enough sunshine, most of the plants died, and the Earth got very cold. According to this theory, the dinosaurs finally became extinct because they could not live without food and warmth, which became scarce as a result of the asteroid.

Like the other theories already mentioned, the asteroid theory has a lot of problems. First, no one knows why this huge space-object would kill every dinosaur (large and small), but leave so many other forms of life unharmed. Why did the asteroid not kill other reptiles, like turtles and alligators? Second, there is nothing in the fossil record that supports the death of all of the dinosaurs at almost the same time. Even though many dinosaurs are found in fossil "graveyards" throughout the world, the fossil record also shows that some lived at a later time. And finally, the collision site in Mexico where some scientists think the asteroid struck [called Chicxulub (CHEEK-shoe-lube)] is very questionable. Although it does appear that an asteroid hit the area, there is no evidence that it caused global destruction.

DINOSAUR GRAVEYARDS AND THE FLOOD

One of the greatest mysteries concerning the dinosaurs is the large number of dinosaur graveyards found in different parts of the world. Dinosaur fossils have been discovered as far north as the Arctic, as far south as Antarctica, and almost everywhere in between. In fact, dinosaur fossils have been found on all seven continents. Nearly 100 years ago, a dinosaur graveyard was found in Tanzania, Africa. Literally tons of fossils and rocks were mined and sent to Berlin, Germany, for display. At Dinosaur National Monument on the Colorado/Utah border, more than 300 dinosaurs of many different kinds have been excavated. Another site in Utah has produced 10,000 dinosaur bones that were extracted from the rock. The burial of such large numbers of dinosaurs in various locations all over the world demands a good answer.

The Dinosaur National Monument fossil quarry (excavation site) is one of the largest fossil "store-houses" in the world, where

over 1,600 fossilized dinosaur bones are buried. Built around the major rock face that contains the fossils is a small museum. The museum offers some interesting information about the early discovery of the monument in 1909. It also propagates the evolutionary theory that dinosaurs lived millions of years ago (as is the case with practically every federally funded dinosaur attraction).

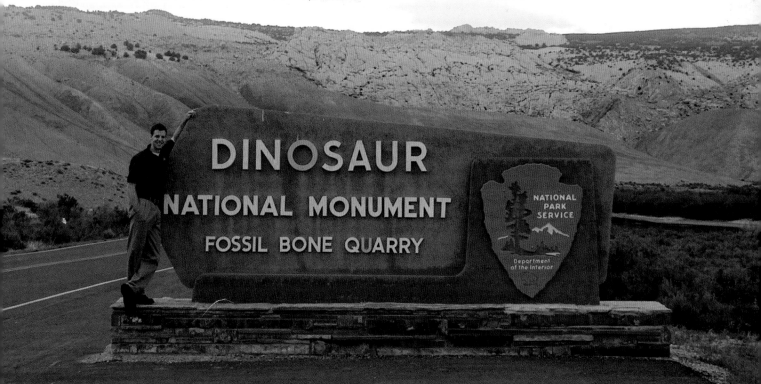

One intriguing thing about the monument is the explanation that is given regarding the cause of this huge fossil graveyard. The wall opposite the rock face contains a large painted mural. This mural shows various dinosaurs wading through deep water. Under the mural, a sign reads: "After a seasonal flood: This scene of 145 million years ago is based on clues found in the rock face behind you. Carcasses brought downstream by the fast-moving, muddy water were washed onto a sandbar. Some were buried completely by tons of sand—their bones preserved in a nearly perfect state."

It is of special interest that such a huge fossil graveyard is said to have occurred because of a "seasonal flood." Further research has

shown that many fossil finds are explained by referencing a seasonal, regional, or flash flood. Most scientists believe that the fossilization of bones usually requires large quantities of water. In November 1999, University of Chicago paleontologist Paul Sereno uncovered a 65-foot-long dinosaur called Jabaria. This skeleton was almost 95% complete. The explanation for its burial? "It looks as though the dinosaurs may have been caught in an ancient flash flood and buried quickly." In an article describing a huge pterosaur graveyard, Robert Sanders stated: "The fossil bones were found strewn throughout an ancient flood deposit in Chile's Atacama des-

ert, suggesting that they were animals or corpses caught up in a flood perhaps 110 million years ago at the beginning of the Cretaceous period."

On a BBC Web site discussing its series "Walking With Dinosaurs," an article explains that much of the information for the first episode of "Walking With Dinosaurs" came from a fossil find called the Ghost Ranch, located near Abaquiu, New Mexico. The text describes this site as one of the richest fossil finds in the world. How does the article explain the fact that so many dinosaurs were buried suddenly? "Palaeontologists believe that the collection of fossils was the result of a mass death around a dwindling water resource during a drought. Before the bodies of the animals were eaten by scavengers, a flash flood buried them in muddy sediments where they were preserved."

How interesting to learn that evolutionists explain many of the largest dinosaur graveyards in the world as having been caused by a flood, though they are quick to include words such as seasonal, flash, regional, and the like. There is no question that such localized disasters have occurred throughout the world, just as they occur today from time to time. But, the problem with these theories is that while they may explain the death of some dinosaurs in some places, they don't adequately explain the existence of dinosaur graveyards throughout the whole world.

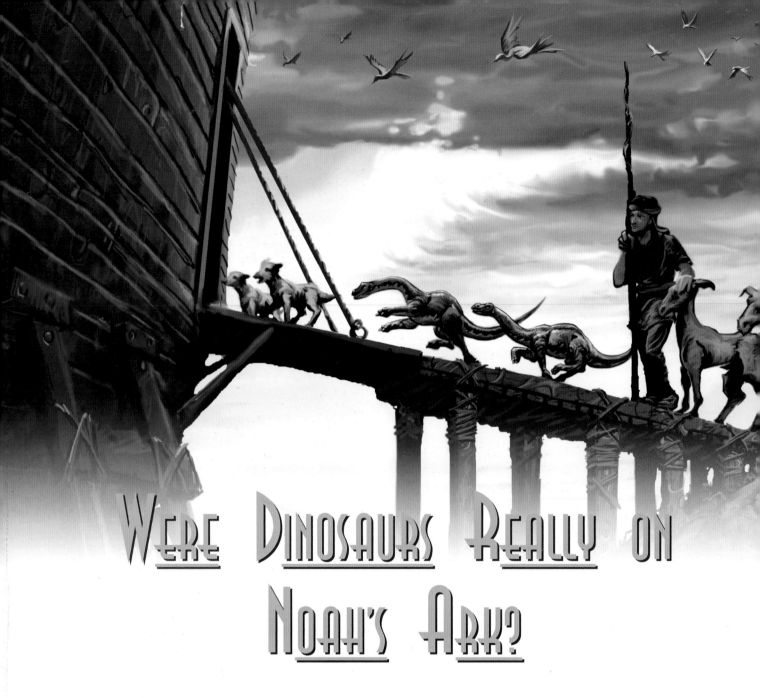

Were Dinosaurs Really on Noah's Ark?

Yes, dinosaurs must have been on Noah's ark! Scientifically, dinosaurs are defined as land-living animals. But the Bible tells us that all land-living animals outside the ark died in the Flood (Genesis 7:21). We know, however, that some dinosaurs must have survived the Flood. Scientific evidence indicates that ancient peoples who lived long after Noah interacted at times with dinosaurs. Also, the book of Job (which was written sometime after the Flood) mentions animals that appear to have been what we call dinosaurs (read Job 40:15-24). The fact that God talked to Job about the behemoth **after the Flood** shows us that dinosaurs were still alive. But how could dinosaurs (which live only on land) have survived the Flood—**unless they were on the ark**?

You might ask, "How did Noah take all of the huge dinosaurs on the ark?" It is important to remember that the ark was a huge vessel—300 cubits long, 50 cubits wide, and 30 cubits high (Genesis 6:15). The word "cubit" comes from a Hebrew word meaning "forearm," because the Hebrews used their forearm in determining the length of a cubit. Generally, a cubit was the distance from the elbow to the tip of the middle finger. According to our own measurements, a cubit would be about 18-20 inches. Thus, the ark was approximately 450 feet long (one-and-a-half football fields!), 75 feet wide, and 45 feet tall. For a long time, it was the largest sea-going vessel ever built.

The ark would have had a total area of about 100,000 square feet—the equivalent of slightly more than 20 standard basketball courts! Its total volume would have been roughly 1,500,000 cubic feet. To get a good idea of just how large the ark really was, creationist John Whitcomb urged people to "imagine waiting at a railroad crossing while 10 freight trains, each pulling 52 boxcars, move slowly by, one after another." Then consider putting all of those boxcars into the ark. The space available inside the ark would have held more than **520 modern railroad boxcars!**

To some people, the idea of dinosaurs on the ark seems absurd. However, it is not so hard to accept when the subject is considered carefully. First, we must remember that God was the Creator of all the animals, and He knew exactly how big the ark needed to be in order to house all the different kinds of land-living animals. Second, contrary to popular belief, not all dinosaurs were massive in size. Many of them were only a few feet tall—even as full-grown adults. Some, in fact, were as small as chickens. And finally, it is very possible that God allowed Noah to take baby dinosaurs into the ark, instead of those that were full grown. That certainly would save a lot of space. From what evidence has been gathered, the largest dinosaur eggs indicate that a 40-foot-long dinosaur laid eggs that were less than a foot in diameter. As hatchlings, even the largest dinosaurs were no bigger than an average house pet. We can see that if the dinosaurs on the ark were young, they would not have needed much more space than the average-size dog.

Fortunately, Noah built the ark exactly as God commanded him, and therefore he had plenty of room for all of the land animals—including the dinosaurs!

DINOSAUR EXTINCTION

So why did dinosaurs eventually become extinct if some survived the Flood? One reason may be that the dinosaurs that survived the Flood on Noah's ark were not able to cope very well in the new world because the climate was so different. One indication that the world was very different after the Flood comes from an understanding of how the ages of people at their deaths decreased by hundreds of years. Before the Flood, the Bible indicates that men lived to be 800 and 900 years old (see Genesis 5:3-32). In fact, the grandfather of Noah, whose name was Methuselah, lived to be 969 years old (that's almost a millennium!). After the Flood, however, people began dying at much younger ages. Instead of living to be 800 or 900 years old, the descendants of Noah eventually began living to be only 150 to 200 years old. For example, Abraham died at age 185 (Genesis 25:7). Although that may sound old to us today, compared to the ages of people before the Flood, it is much younger. Many creation scientists believe that the same conditions that caused man's life span to decrease were the same condi-

tions that eventually (years later) drove the dinosaurs to extinction.

The last surviving dinosaurs may have become extinct for the same reason that many other animals through the years have died out—the filling of our planet with humans. It is very possible that humans hunted various kinds of dinosaurs to extinction. Certain species of tigers, bears, elephants, and hippos have all been hunted almost to the brink of destruction. Perhaps the same thing happened to many kinds of dinosaurs. Immediately after the Flood, God said to Noah and his family:

> The fear of you and the dread of you shall be on every beast of the earth, on every bird of the air, on all that move on the earth, and on all the fish of the sea. They are given into your hand. Every moving thing that lives shall be food for you. I have given you all things, even as the green herbs (Genesis 9:2-3).

It was not until after the Flood that we read of God granting humans permission to hunt animals. Soon, mighty men like Nimrod, a grandson of Ham, began hunting the various animals of the Earth (Genesis 10:8-12). Although dinosaurs did repopulate in various places throughout the world after the Flood, it could be that many eventually died out at the hand of hunters. Countries all over the world have stories of dragon slayers. Perhaps there is at least some truth to them.

FLOOD LEGENDS

After God saved Noah and his family from the Flood, God told them to have children and fill the Earth with people. They obeyed God and had many children and grandchildren. In fact, every one of us today is a relative of Noah and his family. Can you imagine being one of the grandchildren or great grandchildren of Noah? You would have been able to see all the canyons and devastation that the Great Flood caused. You might have even used some of the wood on the ark to build houses or fences. But you would not have seen the Flood. Can you imagine asking your father or grandfather to tell you about the Flood and all the animals on the ark? "What kind of animals did you see, papa? How long did it rain? What happened to all the people who were not on the ark? How did you know the Flood was coming?" These might have been just a few of the questions that you would have asked. Of course, we today can go to the Bible for the answers to those questions, but the people right after the Flood did not have the book of Genesis to read (it was not written until several hundred years after the Flood). The story of the Flood was passed from parents to children for many generations. In about

1500 B.C., God inspired Moses to write the real story of Noah's family in the book of Genesis so the true facts would be recorded for all history.

Before Moses wrote about the Flood, many parents and grandparents were telling their children and grandchildren all about the huge ark, the wonderful animals, and the devastating Flood. As the years went by, they probably altered the story, and the details were changed. Maybe you have played the game called "Gossip." It is a very easy game. Several people get in a circle or a straight line. The person at the beginning of the circle or line thinks of a sentence like "the red horse fell into the water." That person whispers the sentence into the ear of the person next to him. He cannot repeat the sentence after it has been whispered once, and he must talk very softly. The next person in line listens carefully and then whispers the sentence she heard into the ear of the person next to her. After the sentence has gone through every person in the line or circle, the last person repeats the sentence that he was told. Most every time, the sentence at the end of the game is different than what was whispered at the beginning. For instance, the last person in the line might have heard something like "the dead horse turned into the otter" instead of the real sentence, "the red horse fell into the water." The game does a good job of showing that words and sentences can get confused when they are passed from one person to another.

When we look into the history of mankind, we find that there are over 250 legends about a great flood. Nations such as China, Greece, India, Africa, and Mexico all have legends about a huge flood. Some of their details are very different, but in most of the legends animals were saved, one family was chosen, the flood covered the entire Earth, and a boat of some kind was built. When you think about it, that is exactly what we would expect to find if all the nations around the world trace their roots back to Noah and his family. Over the many years, the details of the Flood story were altered, but many facts stayed the same. Aren't we thankful God inspired Moses to write down the correct version of the story so that we can know exactly what happened?

Let's take a look at some of the legends from around the world to see how similar the story of Noah is to many of the other flood legends.

GREECE

According to the Greek legend of the deluge (flood), humans became wicked. Zeus, the leader of the many gods in Greek mythology, wanted to destroy humans by a flood and raise up another race of men. However, before he could do this, a man named Deucalion and his wife Pyrrha were warned of the disaster. This fortunate couple was placed in a large wooden chest by Prometheus, one of the immortals. For nine days and nights the flood waters covered almost all of the Earth. Only a few mountain peaks remained. The wooden chest came to rest on the peak of Mount Parnassus. After leaving the wooden chest, Deucalion and his wife repopulated the Earth by throwing stones that turned into people.

BABYLON

One of the closest matches to the story of Noah comes from the land of Babylon. In a story known as the Gilgamesh Epic, a man named Gilgamesh meets an old man named Utnapishtim. The old man, Utnapishtim, told Gilgamesh how one of the gods had warned the old man to build a boat because a terrible flood was coming. Utnapishtim built the boat and covered it with pitch (a substance like tar that would keep water out). He put animals of all kinds in the boat and also took provisions. He and his family got in the boat, and the flood lasted for six days and nights. When the flood ended, the boat rested on Mount Niser. After seven days, Utnapishtim sent a dove out to see if the waters had gone down. This dove came back, so he sent a swallow. It also returned to the boat. Finally, he sent out a raven that never returned. Utnapishtim and his family left the boat and sacrificed to their gods.

TOLTEC INDIANS

In the ancient land now known as Mexico, one tribe of Indians known as the Toltecs told of a great flood. In their legend, a great flood destroyed the "first world" 1,716 years after it was created. Only a few people escaped this worldwide flood in a "toptlipetlocali," a word that refers to something like a closed chest. After these few people left the "closed chest," they wandered about the Earth and found a location where they built a "zacuali," something like a high tower, in case another flood came upon the Earth. During the time of the "zacuali," their languages were confused and they separated to different places on the Earth.

CHINA

In the land of China, there are many legends about a great flood. One of those comes from a group of people known as the Nosu. According to their legend, God sent a messenger to Earth to warn three sons that a flood was coming. Only the youngest son, Dum, listened to the messenger. He built a wooden boat to prepare for the flood. About 20 days later, a huge flood covered the whole Earth. Dum entered his boat and was saved. The boat landed on the mountains of Tibet, where Dum had three sons who repopulated the Earth.

THE MARKS OF THE FLOOD

Many geologists (scientists who study rocks) say that things happen now just like they happened in the past—an idea known as uniformitarianism [YOU-ni-FOR-muh-TARE-ee-uh-niz-um]. They say that "the present is the key to the past." Here is how this idea works. Suppose that you turned on your water hose in the backyard. The water from the hose begins to erode a small channel through the mud. If you measured how much mud it eroded per minute, then you could calculate how long the water had been running. For instance, if the water eroded one inch of mud every minute, and the channel that was cut through the mud was 20 inches deep, then according to the idea of uniformitarianism, the hose would have been on for 20 minutes. This idea works well to measure some things, but it also has many problems when measuring other things.

For instance, suppose you walk into a yard that has a 30-inch channel running through it, with

water from a hose that is eroding the soil at an inch a minute. You would probably assume the water hose had been running for 30 minutes. You decide to ask the owner of the yard, so you knock on the door. The owner of the yard informs you that firemen had just come by and used their big hose in his yard. It took them two minutes to erode the channel with their great big hose. He also told you that he had only been running his hose for one minute. You see, the problem with the idea of uniformitarianism is that many things happened in the past that are not still happening. The Flood of Noah is a good example of an event that would have caused major miscalculations for those who try to use the idea of uniformitarianism.

Some evolutionists say the little river (called the Colorado River) at the bottom of the Grand Canyon slowly, over millions of years, cut and carved that huge canyon. They say that it took a massive amount of water to form the canyon, and they do not know where else the water could have come from, except that little river. But the Bible tells us that there once was an enormous amount of water that poured down and covered the entire Earth: the Flood of Noah. It not only filled the valleys and plains, but also covered every mountain—even the tallest ones of Noah's day. When the Flood was over, God made the waters recede, and a lot of water was being moved around. This is the amount of water that the scientists say would have been able to carve such a huge hole. So, most likely, the Flood God sent upon the Earth "carved" much of what we know as the Grand Canyon.

Today, we have seen how a large flood can carve out a canyon like the Grand Canyon. On May 18, 1980, the Mount St. Helens volca-

to form in one day, then what would a person expect to happen when the "fountains of the deep" were broken up and the entire world was covered by water (as in Noah's Flood)? Surely, the evidence from Mount St. Helens shows that a huge flood could have caused the Grand Canyon.

erupted. The effects of Mount St. Helens' eruption have cast serious doubt on the long-held theory that the Grand Canyon must have been slowly carved over millions of years. On March 19, 1982, a small eruption around the summit of Mount St. Helens caused a mudflow that was 20 miles long. The flow quickly cut a canyon that was 140 feet deep. The canyon produced by the mudflow has been called "The Little Grand Canyon." It got its name because it appears to be a one-fortieth scale model of the Grand Canyon.

Think about this: If the eruption of Mount St. Helens caused a canyon 1/40th the size of the Grand Canyon

In addition, scientists recently discovered that the island of Britain was formed by a huge flood. In fact, these scientists tell us that it was the biggest flood that any scientist has ever studied. They believe that the megaflood which caused Britain released 35 million cubic feet of water per second, which is 100 times greater than the water that the Mississippi River discharges. (A man named Thomas Wagner wrote about this flood in an article titled "Study: Flooding Left Britain an Island.") The Flood of Noah's day would have been a huge flood that could easily have caused the island of Britain.

After looking at all the evidence, we can see that the Flood recorded in Genesis happened. It is not a myth or an untrue legend. It was a worldwide catastrophe that caused many of the geologic formations we see today. It should also remind us that God is in control.

Conclusion

For many years, people who believe in evolution have tried to use dinosaurs to teach people like you that evolution is true. According to evolutionists, dinosaurs evolved and became extinct millions of years before humans ever existed. Evolutionists have printed beautiful, full-color books trying to convince readers that humans and dinosaurs did not live at the same time. Millions of dollars have been spent by these evolutionists to print books, produce television programs, and create cartoons that present only a few of the real facts about dinosaurs and humans.

It is time that the true story about dinosaurs is heard! The story told by evolutionists does not agree with the true facts of science or the Bible. After looking at all the evidence, it is easy to see that dinosaurs and humans once lived together. Humans painted and carved accurate pictures of these remarkable animals hundreds of years before our modern society began to discover their bones.

Historians like Herodotus wrote about flying reptiles over 2,400 years ago. Even the Bible describes large creatures that sound very much like dinosaurs. But the Bible does not use these creatures to try and teach people evolution. The Bible uses these magnificent creatures to bring glory to the Creator. After all, only God can create animals as remarkable as dinosaurs. God put humans on the Earth with dinosaurs so that humans could look at the dinosaurs and see God's power and ability. We humans have created many wonderful machines and buildings, but we have never been able to design anything as amazing as a dinosaur. Dinosaurs do not "prove" evolution; instead, dinosaurs prove that there is a powerful God who rules the Universe, and only He has the power to design such "terribly great lizards."